Creating an Atmosphere to HEAR God Speak

Robby Gallaty

Creating an Atmosphere to HEAR God Speak
by Robby Gallaty

Printed in the United States of America

ISBN 978-1-60791-696-3

Unless otherwise indicated, Bible quotations are taken from The ESV Version of the Bible. Copyright © 2008 by Crossway Bibles.

Layout and cover design my Jared Callais.
Cover photo taken by Pleasant Vonnoh.

www.xulonpress.com

—⧚⧜⧚—

Pastor Robby Gallaty has recognized and engagingly addressed the "Achilles heel" of most evangelical churches—discipleship. In *Creating an Atmosphere to Hear God Speak,* Brother Gallaty has laid out an exciting and accessible plan for individual Christian spiritual growth that, if followed, will change lives and transform churches.

Dr. Richard Land
President
The Southern Baptist Convention's Ethics &
Religious Liberty Commission

The Spirit of God through the Word of God creates disciples – men and women who not only treasure

Christ but who possess a passion to lead others to treasure Him, as well. Robby Gallaty is one of those men – he knows the Word, he loves the Word, and he delights in leading others to discover its wonder. I eagerly recommend this book as a resource for new Christians and Christians who long to multiply the Word in and through their lives.

Dr. David Platt
Senior Pastor
The Church at Brook Hills

When we lose discipleship, we lose permission to teach people deeply. A disciple is one who chooses to follow Christ in submission to others of a kindred spirit. It is only in that environment where you can "teach them to obey everything Christ commanded." Pastor Gallaty provides a primer for one to get started on this journey. There is no doubt if any follower would apply the message of this book, they won't be able to stop themselves from being a joyful and fruitful disciple.

Bill Hull
Author of *Choose the Life* and
The Disciple Making Pastor

I am delighted to write any word on behalf of my friend and brother, Robby Gallaty. The hand of the Lord is on him in a remarkable way. Robby is a walking example of God's amazing grace, from his wonderful conversion to his distinctive ministry of preaching and evangelism. I am convinced the Lord has raised up a fresh voice that speaks God's Word with an unusual power and anointing. I have no doubt this book will be a blessing to you and I am sure you will want to recommend it to all your friends.

Dr. Don Wilton
Senior Pastor
First Baptist Spartanburg

This book is dedicated to:

Tim LaFleur and David Platt for giving me a burden for making disciples.

Jesse Simoneaux, Jason Galloway, and Jody Blaylock for showing me how to make disciples.

Kandi Gallaty for helping me become a disciple.

ACKNOWLEDGMENTS

—ᗡᑎᗡ—

In the midst of relocating, taking on the role of pastor of a new church, and working on my Ph.D., the Lord gave me the grace to complete this book. I am grateful for His strength and sustenance throughout this project. I would also like to express my deep appreciation for those who have assisted me in accomplishing the completion of this book. I am thankful for Tammy Barber, Ken Kendall, and Kay Marie Kendall for reviewing the manuscript and examining its integrity. I could not have completed the book without their input.

I am thankful for David Platt and Tim LaFleur who exposed me to the basics of discipleship. I am grateful for Jody Blaylock, Jesse Simoneaux, and Jason Galloway who met with me every Friday for lunch while I was pastoring Immanuel Baptist Church. Through trial and error and through our own discipleship group, we learned what worked and what didn't work. I would not be where I am without my parents, Bob and Margaret, and my sister, Lori, who believed in me when no one else did. Finally, I am grateful for my wife Kandi who motivates me everyday to be a better husband, father, and follower of Christ.

CONTENTS

FOREWORD

It is my joy to recommend *Creating an Atmosphere to HEAR God Speak* by Robby Gallaty. Robby is a young man of sterling character with a deep, steadfast commitment to Jesus Christ. It certainly has been wonderful to see him grow in ministry and to become one of God's choice servants.

Several summers ago, I challenged Robby to make disciples, and, in the mountains near Santa Fe, I modeled what that might look like. He took to that challenge whole-heartedly. In addition to becoming a powerful preacher, he has developed a sincere passion for discipleship and pours his life into faithful men.

This book contains a four-fold strategy to help believers connect with God and His Word—hearing it by reading, hiding it in their hearts by memorizing, honoring it through prayer, and helping by obeying the Word. It is birthed out of a deep burden to help believers, especially new ones, truly connect with God. I earnestly and enthusiastically recommend this valuable resource to anyone who wants to hear God speak!

Tim LaFleur
Teaching Pastor - First Baptist Thibodaux
Campus Minister - Nicholls State University

PREFACE

O n November 22, 1999, my life was radically changed. While driving home from work, an 18-wheeler rear-ended me at sixty-five miles an hour. Two discs in my neck and two in my back were herniated as a result of the accident. Consequently, the doctors prescribed pharmaceutical drugs to deal with the pain; within three months, I was addicted to pain medicine. After a three-year battle with drugs and two rehabilitation treatments, I cried out to the Lord Jesus for help. On November 12, 2002, I surrendered my life completely to Christ. For a copy of my testimony or to access resources to assist in becoming a disciple or making disciples, visit our website at www.awordfromhisword.org.

Without a church to attend or a mentor in the faith, I had no direction in how to grow closer to God. No one instructed me in the value of reading the Bible or spending time with God. Yes, I heard sermons about these disciplines from the pastor of the church I was attending, but instructions in the form of these practices were nonexistent. If I could have had a simple book outlining the fundamentals for growth in the Christian life, it would have helped immensely. A manual teaching the basics of Scripture reading, Scripture memorization, prayer, and obedience could have eliminated countless days wandering aimlessly as a Christian. Many believers, if not most, do not know the need or understand how, to study the Bible, memorize Scripture, pray, and obey God's Word. Many of those who do know these disciplines rarely practice them. This was the motivation for writing this book.

Robby Gallaty
Chattanooga, Tennessee
March 2009

INTRODUCTION

———〰〰———

As a child whenever conversations of spring-cleaning filled the air, I looked for anything to occupy my time other than cleaning the garage. If your parents were anything like mine, once a year they would rise early on a Saturday morning and reorganize the shed behind our house. When I was old enough to assist, my help was not an option, but a necessity. The first year my hard work paid off. After removing the lawnmower, weed-eater, motorbikes, and bicycles, a massive black box caught my attention from the back corner. Climbing over mattresses and old dressers to get there, I carefully exited the shed without dropping my new found treasure. "What is it, Dad?" I asked. He bent down, wiped the dust off, and with a smile on his face responded, "This is the world radio I had when I was your age." The device was fascinating to me.

Unfortunately for my Dad's sake, we spent the remainder of the day cleaning the radio and not the garage. Later that night we gathered around that radio and with fingers crossed, we plugged the cord into the outlet. To my Dad's surprise and mine, it worked just as it did twenty years ago. Although the naked ear could not hear the radio frequencies being transmitted through the air, stations from China, France, and Europe could be tuned in with a careful turn of the dial. As I think back to that day, I am conscious of the fact that God is speaking to us every day, but we are unable to hear his voice without the proper atmosphere. His voice, like the radio frequencies, is being projected through many different avenues to his children. All believers would admit that hearing from the Lord is a high priority; however, incorporating this into one's life is an elusive concept.

I have learned that the secrets to the Christian life are the obvious things. While I would love to uncover some hidden truth never before discovered, God has already communicated in his Word everything we need for growth. The Apostle Paul told the Church at Rome, **"So faith comes from hearing, and hearing through the *word* of Christ"** (Romans 10:17).[1] After spending the last six years of my life being discipled and discipling others, I have identified four disciplines for spiritual development. It is important to note that these are not the only four disciplines an individual may incorporate into his or her life, but these four practices are necessary for spiritual growth. And these practices do provide a springboard for other disciplines to flourish—evangelism, solitude, frugality, fasting, Scripture meditation, and worship. For instance, when a believer is studying the Word, the desire for evangelism will grow, the desire for fasting will grow, the desire for worship will grow, and so on.

The four disciplines or pillars that support the mantel of discipleship are:

1. **H.E.A.R.ing** from God's Word (reading)
2. **Hiding** (memorization)
3. **Honoring** (prayer)
4. **Helping** (obedience)

Each discipline complements the others. Integrating them individually will increase spiritual fervor; collectively, they will produce exponential growth in one's life. Whether you are a new convert or a believer raised your entire life in church, this fourfold plan will produce tangible results for anyone disciplined enough to stick with it. The disciplines are meant to be practiced with a group of individuals, mainly for accountability, but they can be used alone.

The entire system is reproducible. In fact, it should be reproduced. Jesus commanded his followers to go into the world and **"make disciples"** (Matthew 28:19). He follows this command by providing instruction for developing disciples: **"teaching them** [future disciples] **to observe all that I have commanded you"** (Matthew 28:20). The first and foremost way to make disciples is to become one, and the only way to effectively teach others is to continue as a lifelong learner. We are closest to Christ when we are doing what he has commanded us to do.

1

H. E. A. R.
Reading the Word

—⌇⌇⌇—

"All Scripture is breathed out by God and profitable for teaching, for reproof, for correction, and for training in righteousness, that the man of God may be competent, equipped for every good work."
2 Tim. 3:16-17

Why should I read the Bible?

One of the goals of getting in shape is to produce lean muscle mass. Eating six good meals a day provides high amounts of protein, causing the metabolism to work overtime. When I was serious about working out, I ate a regular diet of eggs, tuna, eggs, chicken, eggs, turkey, and eggs. The last item I wanted to enter my mouth was a chocolate candy bar. Why? Because what I put into my body was going to manifest itself on the outside in the form of a displeasing physique. If I wanted to generate positive results, my food intake had to be healthy. Subsequently, our spiritual body is the same way. If we would not go a day without eating three meals, why have we convinced ourselves that we can do that with spiritual nutrition? Daily Bible intake is the equivalent of food for the body—without it we will starve. Many church members are malnourished believers who rarely, if ever, read the Word other than on Sunday at church.

Discipleship is the process of being conformed to the image of Christ through obedience to the will of God. A heart that obeys God is a heart that has first come to love Him. In order to love God, you must

know Him intimately. A heart that knows God is a heart
that has been transformed by the renewing of the mind
through the study and application of God's Word.

Jesus' first experience after His baptism provides
proof for why we need a daily intake of God's Word.
Matthew records the temptation of Jesus in chapter 4:

> **Then Jesus was led up by the Spirit into the
> wilderness to be tempted by the devil. And
> after fasting forty days and forty nights,
> he was hungry. And the tempter came and
> said to him, "If you are the Son of God,
> command these stones to become loaves
> of bread." But he answered, "It is written,
> 'Man shall not live by bread alone, but by
> every word that comes from the mouth of
> God'"** (Matthew 4:1-4).

Jesus, with the backdrop of the Exodus account
in his mind, makes an important connection. The
book of Exodus records the account of a man named
Moses, whom God chose to lead the Israelites out
from bondage under the rule of Pharaoh and into the
land that He had promised them. Through a series

of demonstrations of God's sovereign power, the Israelites were allowed to leave Egypt and flee to the desert.

Without food or water, they were forced to rely on God for daily sustenance. After the people complained to Moses about the absence of food, God spoke about his provision for life.

> **Then the LORD said to Moses, "Behold, I am about to rain bread from heaven for you, and the people shall go out and gather a day's portion every day, that I may test them, whether they will walk in my law or not. On the sixth day, when they prepare what they bring in, it will be twice as much as they gather daily"** (Exodus 16:4-5).

The following day God provided food for the people in the form of manna (bread). Having seen the flaky substance on the ground, the people asked if this was the bread that God had promised.

And Moses said to them, "It is the bread that the LORD has given you to eat. This is what the LORD has commanded: 'Gather of it, each one of you, as much as he can eat. You shall each take an omer [2 liters], according to the number of the persons that each of you has in his tent.'" And the people of Israel did so. They gathered, some more, some less. But when they measured it with an omer, whoever gathered much had nothing left over, and whoever gathered little had no lack. Each of them gathered as much as he could eat. And Moses said to them, "Let no one leave any of it over till the morning." But they did not listen to Moses. Some left part of it till the morning, and it bred worms and stank... (Exodus 16:15-20).

There are two important principles about spiritual nourishment that are applicable to our lives found in this text. First, the people were forced to gather their own bread each day. They physically had to make time and expend effort to gather food. Secondly, the bread that was gathered was only good for that particular day. The process had to be repeated each day, except on the Sabbath. Yesterday's manna is not

sufficient for today, and today's manna is not sufficient for tomorrow.

How is this passage connected to Jesus' words in Matthew 4:4?

Jesus connects the bread, something Jewish
people would remember as the source for sustenance
in that dry desert, with the Word of God. Every day
you must set aside time for spiritual replenishment.
Additionally, what you read today is not sufficient
for tomorrow, and tomorrow's reading is only going
to satisfy you for that day. Scripture intake builds
upon the previous day's reading. This is the reason
for a consistent, systematic quiet time. In summary,
you must set aside a time everyday with God for the
private study of His Word.

What are some common excuses?

People come up with a multitude of excuses as to why they do not read the Bible. This semester I flew back and forth to seminary every week for class. Every trip I would ask the person sitting next to me on the plane the same question: "Why do you believe people are not reading the Bible? Or for that matter, why aren't you reading the Bible?" The most common responses were: "I don't have enough time." "It doesn't have any bearing on my life." "I don't know what it means." "The Bible is confusing to me." "It is too old." "I have read it before and didn't get anything out of it." The most revealing excuse that I heard was: "It doesn't speak to me." Polling the passengers on the plane caused me to question my own quiet time.

After honest examination, I realized that my own quiet time bordered on the edge of becoming routine and mundane even after a few years. In an attempt for creativity, I have integrated different Bible reading plans over the years to foster a new interest in studying the Word. Reading one Old Testament passage, one New Testament passage, and one of the Psalms every day was a plan that I began to use. However, after awhile, I found myself more interested in checking off boxes in my reading plan each day than hearing from God.

One year, I started a plan of reading through the books of Scripture consecutively. This plan worked for awhile but became difficult when I came to Leviticus. As I read the assigned portion, I found myself dozing off or thinking about upcoming appointments or meetings from the previous day. Another plan was to read the Old Testament once and the New Testament twice during the course of a year. For the most part, every plan accomplished its purpose, which was to read through the Bible in a year, but fell short of God's purpose. After much prayer, I realized that the problem was not in the reading plan, but in the reader. I found that I was not looking for or listening for a word from God, nor was I looking for ways to apply the truth of the Word and to incorporate it into my life. What I needed was a plan that would help develop an atmosphere where I could hear from God.

How do I have a quiet time?

You *must* have a daily quiet time. It is essential for spiritual development. This can be done early in the morning or at night. Many suggest waking up early in the morning to study by citing the over-whelming number of Scripture passages that recommend it. The Psalms, for example, speak of rising early in the morning to communicate to God (See

Psalms 5 and 88). Likewise, Jesus rose early in the morning for intimate communion with His Father (Mark 1:35). Personally, I study at night. It is a time for me to replay the events of the day, take every thought captive, and focus on the Lord. Two men that I mentored spent every morning before work in their vehicles alone with God. The point is that you must have a selected time and place for isolated devotional time with God. If the atmosphere is noisy or congested, how will you hear from God?

In order to grow in your quiet time, it is helpful to have a plan. When my wife, Kandi, and I go on vacation every year, we get on the internet and download directions to our destination. These directions provide step-by-step instructions for an easy arrival. A mapped-out trip saves a lot of headaches along the way and so does a planned reading schedule. Similarly, it takes planning to become a disciple of Christ.

When I was a new believer, I used the OPRA technique. I would randomly OPEN the Bible, POINT to a passage, READ the verse, and try to APPLY it to my life. Thankfully, I didn't land on the Scripture that says, "He [speaking of Judas Iscariot] went and hanged himself" (Matthew 27:5). Opening to random Scriptures will not provide solid biblical growth any more than eating random foods out of your pantry will provide solid physical growth.

An effective reading plan is required. While there are many plans out there, it is important to find one that works for you and stick to it (Appendix 5 contains a sample Bible reading plan). In order to get familiar with this plan, I generally recommend beginning with the second book of Timothy.

The Apostle Paul wrote to Timothy, his disciple, about important, applicable truths for the Christian life. Since the book of 2 Timothy is relatively small, only four chapters, it can be read in its entirety every day. Begin the first day by reading all four chapters. Continue with the same process every day. At the end of seven days, you will have read through the entire book seven times. By continuously reading through the book, you will be able to move beyond mere casual reading and begin to uncover the applicable truth of the book. Words that might be glossed over in casual reading will begin to come alive with each additional reading.

The H.E.A.R. reading outline explained below encourages the reader to read with a life-transforming purpose. No longer will the focus be on finishing in order to check-off a box; rather, the purpose will be to read in order to understand and respond. The acronym H.E.A.R. stands for **HIGHLIGHT**, **EXPLAIN**, **APPLY**, and **RESPOND**. Each step is a piece of the puzzle that creates an atmosphere to hear God speak to us.

How much time should I spend?

At this point, the question of time arises. We should not put parameters on God. I have spent as short as 5 minutes alone with the Lord and as long as a few hours poring over the Scriptures. Since God is not bound by time, let us be free of putting a time restraint on Him. Remember, what you put into something determines what you get out of it. The same goes for your quiet time. A quiet time is more than reading. There is also the aspect of waiting on God to speak and listening to Him. He allowed the Israelites to wander forty years in the desert in order to teach them a lesson on humility. **"Remember how the LORD your God led you all the way in the desert these forty years, to humble you and to test you in order to know what was in your heart, whether or not you would keep his commands"** (Deuteronomy 8:2, NIV). Keep in mind that God is not in a rush and you shouldn't be either.

What is a good translation?

The answer is this: the one that gets read. Many who argue for a particular translation over another may never read the one they are proposing. Overall, any translation that you will read and study is a good translation.

How do I begin Hearing from God?

After settling on a reading plan and securing a time for study, you are ready to *H.E.A.R.* from God (Our first small group initially used the Life Journal, but decided to create a method more suitable to our needs).[1] Let's assume that you begin your quiet time with the book of 2 Timothy, and today's reading is the first chapter of the book. Before reading the text, ask God to speak to you. This may seem like a given, but there have been countless times that I have had to stop in the middle of reading and ask the Lord's forgiveness for not asking Him to speak to me through His Word. The Bible speaks of needing spiritual assistance to understand the truths of God. **"The natural person does not accept the things of the Spirit of God, for they are folly to him, and he is not able to understand them because they are spiritually discerned"** (1 Corinthians 2:14). It is imperative that we seek God's guidance in order to understand His Word.

Prior to reading, open your notebook or journal, and at the top left hand corner, write the letter H (Appendix 1 contains an example of a completed H.E.A.R. entry). This will remind you to read with a purpose. In the course of your reading, there will probably be one or two verses that speak to you. After reading the designated portion, **HIGHLIGHT** each verse that speaks to you by copying it under the letter H. Write out the following:

- The name of the book

- The chapter and verse numbers

- The verse

- A word to describe the passage

This will make it easier to find the passage when you want to revisit it in the future.

After you have Highlighted the passage, write the letter E under the previous entry. At this stage you will **EXPLAIN** what the text means. This is accomplished by asking a series of questions. You are not able to interview the writer of the book of 2 Timothy, so you must ask questions to uncover its meaning. The context of the passage holds the meaning of the text.

A. Berkeley Mickelsen in his book *Interpreting the Bible* states, "By observing what precedes and what follows a passage, the interpreter has a greater opportunity to see what the writer was seeking to convey to his original readers. These readers did not plunge into the middle of the letter and seize out a few consecutive sentences. They read carefully the whole document.... 'A text without a context is just a pretext.' Faithful adherence to context will create in the interpreter a genuine appreciation for the authority of Scripture."[2] The context of a passage uncovers the meaning behind the text.

Some questions to stimulate thought might be these:

- Why was this written?
- Why did the Holy Spirit include this passage in the book?
- What is he intending to communicate through this text?
- What does the text mean?

Remember, at this point there are no right or wrong answers to these questions. You are beginning the process of discovering the specific and personal word that God has for you. What is important is that you are engaging the text and wrestling with its meaning.

After writing a short summary of what you think the text means, write the letter A below the letter E. Under the A, write the word **APPLY**. This is the heart of the process. Everything culminates under this heading. As you have done before, ask a series of questions to uncover the significance of these verses to you. Some questions to consider are as follows:

- How can this help me?
- What does this mean today?
- What would the application of this verse look like in my life?
- What does this mean to me?

These questions bridge the gap between the ancient world and today's world. They also provide a way for God to speak to you regarding the application of His Word. Your answers can range from two sentences to five sentences. Challenge yourself to write more than one and no more than five sentences because there is another section to fit on the page.

Finally, below the first three entries write the letter R for **RESPOND**. This response may take on many forms. You may write a call to action. You may describe how you will be different because of it? You may indicate what you are going to do because of what you have learned? You may respond with a petition to the Lord by writing out a prayer to God. For example, you may ask God to help you to be more loving or you may ask God to give you a desire to be more generous in your giving. Keep in mind that this is your response to what you have just read.

Notice that all of the words are in the present tense and active voice—**HIGHLIGHT**, **EXPLAIN**, **APPLY**, and **RESPOND.** This gives the sense of action. Instead of waiting passively, God desires for us to actively pursue Him. Jesus stated, **"Ask, and it will be given to you; seek, and you will find; knock, and it will be opened to you"** (Matthew 7:7).

Evangelist Robert L. Sumner in his book *The Wonder of the Word of God* tells the challenging story of a man in Kansas City who was badly injured in an explosion. After losing his eyesight and the use of both hands, the man was greatly distraught, for he could never read the Bible again. His distress was turned into joy after hearing of a woman in England who read Braille with her lips. He searched and found a copy of the Bible in Braille. Sadly, he was discouraged again when he realized the nerve endings in his lips were too damaged to recognize the characters of the pages. One day as he lifted the raised lettering up to his lips, his tongue touched a few of the letters. He thought to himself, "I could read the Bible with my tongue."[3]

At the time of writing, Robert Sumner reported that the man had read through the entire Bible four times with his tongue. Prayerfully, this man will not be standing next to you when you arrive in heaven. In comparison, there will be no excuse for laziness in regards to reading or memorizing the Word (Appendix 3 describes a method for reading, studying, memorizing, and applying the Word).

SUGGESTED READING

Gordon D. Fee and Douglas Stuart, *How to Read the Bible for All Its Worth* 3rd ed. (Grand Rapids, MI: Zondervan, 1981; 2003).

Gordon D. Fee and Douglas Stuart, *How to Read the Bible Book by Book: A Guided Tour* (Grand Rapids, MI: Zondervan, 2002).

Kay Arthur, *How to Study Your Bible: The Lasting Rewards of the Inductive Approach* (Eugene, OR: Harvest House Publishers, 1992).

A. Berkeley Mickelsen, *Interpreting the Bible* (Grand Rapids, MI: Eerdmans Publishing, 1972).

Chad Brand, Charles Draper, and Archie England, *Holman Illustrated Bible Dictionary* (Nashville, TN: Holman Bible Publishers, 1998).

James Strong, *The New Strong's Exhaustive Concordance* (Nashville, TN: Thomas Nelson, 1990).

William D. Mounce, *Mounce's Complete Expository Dictionary of Old and New Testament Words* (Grand Rapids, MI: Zondervan, 2006).

Spiros Zodhiates, *The Complete Word Study Dictionary: Old Testament* (Chattanooga, TN: AMG Publishers, 1993).

Spiros Zodhiates, *The Complete Word Study Dictionary: New Testament* (Chattanooga, TN: AMG Publishers, 1992).

2

Hiding
Memorizing the Word

———∿∿∿———

*"I have stored up your word in my heart,
that I might not sin against you."*

Psalm 119:11

Why memorize Scripture?

Isn't Scripture reading alone good enough? Why should I take the time to memorize passages of the Bible? Isn't Scripture memorization for kids? There is an unfortunate attitude that has manifested itself in churches today when a child enters "big church." It seems that the discipline of Scripture memory practiced as a child is abandoned.

While a regular quiet time opens our ears to hear from God, Scripture memory focuses our minds on the Word of God. Colossians 3:2 says, **"Set your mind on things that are above, not on things that are on earth."** The New Living Translation says, **"Let heaven fill your thoughts."** A pastor from New Orleans spoke these words to me every time he saw me: *"Get into the Word until the Word gets into you."* John says, **"In the beginning was the Word, and the Word was with God and the Word was God.... And the Word became flesh and dwelt among us..."** (John 1:1, 14). Therefore, Jesus was the physical expression of the Word of God; in essence, he was the walking Word.

Moreover, when we saturate our minds with the Word of God, our minds are renewed. Psalm 1 explains the importance of meditating on and memorizing Scripture. **"Blessed is the man who walks not in the counsel of the wicked, nor stands in the way of sinners, nor sits in the seat of scoffers; but his delight is in the law of the LORD, and on his law he meditates day and night."** Paul, knowing this Scripture by heart, taught the Roman church the motivation for renewing the mind, **"Do not be conformed to this world, but be transformed by the renewal of your mind, that by testing you may discern what is the will of God, what is good and acceptable and perfect"** (Romans 12:2). God's will for our lives is uncovered through a regular diet of Scripture reading and memorization.

The renewing of our mind transforms us by focusing our attention on Godly principles. God unfolds His secret to success to Joshua: **"This Book of the Law shall not depart from your mouth, but you shall meditate on it day and night, so that you may be careful to do according to all that is**

written in it. For then you will make your way prosperous, and then you will have good success" (Joshua 1:8). By delighting in the law [Word] of the Lord (Scripture reading), and meditating on His law [Word] day and night (Scripture memory), our lives look less like the world and more like Christ.

What does meditation mean?

When someone uses the word *meditation*, some may tend to think of New Age practices: yoga, transcendental meditation, relaxation techniques, or practices of quieting the mind so the spirit can transcend the body. One popular New Age approach is to quiet the ripples of the soul in order to think of nothing.[1] In contrast, Biblical meditation is not turning the lights off and spending hours pondering nothing. It is not mental passivity, but active mental activity. Through meditation a believer focuses on the Word, ponders the Word, savors the Word, and delights in the Word.

48

The Hebrew word for *meditate* is to murmur or mutter. Jewish people think in visual pictures, so the author of Psalm 1 uses the image is of a pigeon cooing.[2] It is that repetitious noise the bird makes over and over. What does that look like today? The picture is of a man or woman meditating or murmuring the Scriptures over and over in his or her mind. In Israel it is not uncommon to observe a Jewish Rabbi walking with his head down talking to himself. He is reciting from memory the Torah [Old Testament Scripture] portion for the day. Such memorization affords the opportunity to contemplate God's Word anytime and anywhere.

Scripture memorization fills your life with God's Word. Donald Whitney, in his book *Spiritual Disciplines for the Christian Life,* uses the illustration of a hot cup of tea to describe the importance of Scripture memory. Whitney comments, "You are the cup of hot water and the intake of Scripture is represented by the tea bag. Hearing God's Word is like one dip of the tea bag into the cup. Some of the tea's flavor is absorbed by the water, but not as much as would occur with a more thorough soaking of the bag." He adds, "In this analogy, reading, studying, and *memorizing* God's Word are represented by additional plunges of the tea bag into the cup. The more frequently the tea enters the water, the more effect it has."[3] As the flavor of the tea is expelled into the water until the color is tainted with a reddish tint, so should our lives be saturated with the Word until the pages of Scripture distinctively mark us.

How do I memorize Scripture?

There are many systems for committing Scripture to memory. While each is effective in its own right, I have adopted a system that is easy to use and easy to duplicate. Since repetition is the mother of learning, the Scripture memory packs utilize this principle

(Appendix 2 identifies fifteen Scriptures for study). The Scripture verse for study is written on one side of a small white card. On the opposite side of the card, the Scripture reference is recorded. If you are studying Luke 9:23, for example, you would write the verse on one side of the card: **"If anyone would come after me, let him deny himself and take up his cross daily and follow me."** On the opposite side of the card, write the reference Luke 9:23. Insert the card into the window side of the packet. The window contains the verse for study, while the inside pockets are for blank cards.

The system is very simple. Throughout the day the pack should be pulled out for reviewing and studying. The reference should be read first followed by the verse. Continue to recite the verse until you get a feel for the flow of the verse. When you are comfortable with the text, look only at the reference side of the card in order to test your recall.

It is important to recite the reference first, then the verse, and finish with the reference again. This keeps you from becoming a concordance cripple. As a new believer, I was forced to look up every verse in the concordance at the back of my Bible. Whenever I quoted a Scripture to someone I was witnessing to, he would ask me, "Where did you get that from?" My only response was, "Somewhere in the Bible." How can you speak with authority without quoting both the Scripture and verse?

There is a story told of a lady in a small town who had a picturesque garden in the front of her house. Her neighbors admired the garden as they drove by everyday. One day when she was out spreading mulch on her rose bed, a passerby rolled the window down and commented, "You must have a green thumb?" Without hesitation she replied, "No. I have a purple thumb and two bruised knees." Hard work was required to produce a beautiful garden, and memorizing Scripture requires a similar effort.

Scripture memory is difficult. This is one of the reasons why many believers know so few Scriptures. When I was memorizing Greek words in my Introductory Greek class, I learned a valuable secret for getting words to stick in my mind. If I studied the words prior to going to bed, my retention rate was higher the following day because it was the last thing on my mind before I went to bed. When we get to heaven, God is not going to be impressed with how many sports statistics we know by heart, how many television shows we have watched, or how many words of popular songs we can recite. On the other hand, He will be overjoyed with the time we have spent on committing His Word to memory. When we hide His Word in our hearts, we are saying to God, "Your Word is important to me."

Recently, after speaking on this topic, someone commented, "I am just too old to memorize Scripture." My response to them was: "I would rather you spend one year working on one verse than to stand before Christ with none." Despite the difficulty with Scripture memory, will you invest the time needed to hide God's word in your heart? Will you put aside the computer, internet, and television to spend time pondering Scriptures? Thomas Watson, Puritan pastor and teacher, commented, "The reason we come away so cold from reading the Word is because we do not warm ourselves at the fire of meditation."[4]

Where should I start?

A few questions that commonly arise are familiar to us: "What verses should we memorize?" or "Where do I begin?" In order to eliminate excuses, Scripture memory cards have been provided at the back of the book. Whether you are a new convert or a longtime follower of Christ, these fifteen verses will be edifying for any believer. Additionally, they will serve as a model for future memory cards.

Imagine for a moment that you have died and have gone to heaven. As you approach the entrance, you are stopped at the gate and given instructions. To your surprise, heaven is a place where only Scripture is quoted. Nothing can be said apart from the Word of God. You think to yourself, "Thankfully, I brought my Bible with me." Wrong. There are no Bibles in heaven. In fact, the only access to Scripture is through the reciting of verses that you hid in your heart on earth.

How many would you be able to speak? If all that you could speak would be Scripture, would you have anything to say? Everyone would be walking around quoting John 3:16: "For GOD so loved the world." "For God SO loved the world." For God so LOVED the world." God would ask, "Do you know any other

Scriptures?" You may respond with the shortest verse in the Bible, "Jesus wept." Sadly, I believe Jesus is weeping today over the lack of Scriptures that many of his so-called disciples have committed to memory. Let this not be said of your life.

SUGGESTED READING

Donald Whitney, *Spiritual Disciplines for the Christian Life* (Colorado Springs, CO: NavPress, 1994).

Dallas Willard, *The Spirit of the Disciplines: Understanding How God Changes Lives* (San Francisco, CA: HarperCollins Publishers, 1990).

Richard Foster, *Celebration of Discipline: The Path to Spiritual Growth* 3rd ed. (San Francisco, CA: HarperCollins Publishers, 1978; 1998).

3

Honoring
Praying to God

—⦿—

*"And rising very early in the morning, while
it was still dark, he departed and went out to
a desolate place, and there he prayed."*
Mark 1:35

Is prayer important?

Since becoming a believer, I have always under-
stood the importance of prayer, but it wasn't
until I pastored my first church that I developed a
passion for it. Jody visited our church one Sunday
morning, and after the service, asked if I would be

interested in praying with him. He invited me to meet him at 7:30 a.m. in the McDonald's parking lot. I thought we were going to have a cup of coffee, eat an Egg McMuffin, and talk for awhile—I thought wrong. After I spotted his vehicle in the parking lot, he motioned me over to his car. After asking if we could include his prayer partner, he called Doug on his cell phone, and the three of us entered into a time of prayer.

We never made it into the restaurant that day, for the prayer time lasted almost an hour. After finishing his prayer, Jody concluded by saying, "Okay, brother, I will see you next week." I walked back to my truck saying to myself, "What about the coffee and Egg McMuffin?" For the next four months, we prayed together every Monday morning at 7:30 a.m. Later, because of changes in our schedules, it was necessary to pray together by phone rather than in the parking lot.

Wanting to include others in this special time, we randomly called people on a three-way call and asked, "Brother, how can we pray for you today?" After exchanging our requests, each of us offered petitions and supplications to the Lord. Over time, our prayers shifted from asking God to fulfill our spiritual checklist and focused instead on listening to the things important to God. When was the last time you asked the Lord to reveal the things that mattered to Him? We are quick to ask for our needs, but rarely do we ask for God's perspective.

How can I grow in my prayer life?

Andrew Murray spoke on the practice of prayer in his book *With Christ in the School of Prayer*. He comments, "Reading a book about prayer, listening to lectures and talking about it is very good, but it won't teach you to pray. You get nothing without exercise, without practice. I might listen for a year to a professor of music playing the most beautiful music, but that won't teach me to play an instrument."[1] A powerful prayer life is developed through the practice of actually praying. I learned how to pray by praying with others.

Like any spiritual discipline, prayer is a learned behavior. Throughout His earthly ministry, Jesus taught his disciples many things, but Luke 11 captures the first and only time in Scripture when the disciples asked Jesus for instruction on a specific activity.[2] First, notice what they did not choose. Systematic theology was not their first choice. Church growth, leadership, Bible study, and study of the end times were not at the top of the list either. There was not an interest in healing, preaching, singing, or walking on water. Why? The disciples knew that prayer was the source of all things. Of all the courses they could have chosen to be taught by Jesus Himself, they chose the discipline of prayer. By watching Jesus' commitment to spending time with His Father, they were eager to learn how to pray as He prayed.

Jesus starts by giving them what is known as the Lord's Prayer. He bookends this passage with a reference to the Father. In verse 2 of Luke 11, He starts with, **"Father, hallowed be your name,"** and ends in verse 13 with **"...how much more will the heavenly Father give the Holy Spirit to those who ask him!"** One way to radically change your prayer life is to start referring to God as *Dad*.

The passage is embedded with another word about the character of God: "friend." Jesus, providing a visual image for our understanding, tells a parable about three friends.

> **Which of you who has a friend will go to him at midnight and say to him, "Friend, lend me three loaves, for a friend of mine has arrived on a journey, and I have nothing to set before him;" and he will answer from within, "Do not bother me; the door is now shut, and my children are with me in bed.**

**I cannot get up and give you anything?"
I tell you, though he will not get up and
give him anything because he is his friend,
yet because of his impudence he will rise
and give him whatever he needs...** (Luke
11:5-8).

Jesus goes on to say, **"And I tell you, ask, and
it will be given to you; seek, and you will find;
knock, and it will be opened to you"** (Luke 11:9).
We should approach God as both our Father and
friend, but more importantly, we must be persistent
in our prayer time, expecting God to respond to our
requests. Prayer not only brings us into God's presence, it also invites God into our lives. There are
two areas of prayer that are essential: private prayer
and partnership prayer. In order to have an effective
prayer life, you need both.

Private prayer

How long should I pray?

An easy-to-remember formula for prayer is called 7-Up. Pray every morning for the next 7 days for 7 minutes, hence, the name 7-Up (7 days, 7 minutes, when you wake up). It is important to note the time that you begin in order to monitor your progress. Most of those who have accepted the challenge initially respond by saying, "I prayed for myself, my friends, my family, and everyone else I could think of. I was sure that I prayed for at least 10 minutes, but after looking at the clock, only four minutes had passed." If you have never spent 7 minutes in prayer, it will be challenging at first. This will reveal just how little time you spend alone with the Lord.

Another suggestion is to keep a list of five specific prayer requests in a prayer log (Appendix 4 has an example of a prayer log). Just as the Israelites erected spiritual stones marking the movement of the Lord

(Joshua 4), your prayer log is a way of praising the Lord for His responding to your requests. Whether your desire is for a family member to enter into a relationship with Jesus or for personal guidance from God, it is helpful to write these desires down. In addition to recording the requests in a journal, you should record the date you made the request and the date it was answered. After the Lord answers a request, it is important to add another to the list. This is essential because it gives you the opportunity to rejoice for answered prayers as well as to provide a testimony to tell others of God's goodness (putting a spiritual stone in the ground, if you will). Sharing your journal will encourage others to pray as well.

What should I pray for?

The Lord's Prayer starts with the character and person of God. The Psalms speak of His holiness, righteousness, sovereignty, and love. After focusing on God, pray for the person who needs it most—you. Before you can help others, you yourself must be at peace with God. Next, pray for those who are closest to you, such as your spouse, your children, and your family. Then, pray for your church family, friends, and co-workers. It is also helpful to get into the habit of praying Scripture. There are numerous passages containing prayers by the Apostle Paul that can be applied to your life (i.e., Ephesians 1:15-23, 3:14-21; Colossians. 1:11-14). Praying Scripture includes not only praying actual prayers from the Scripture, but also communicating back to God the language of Scripture regarding His character, His promises, and His love.

Partnership prayer

When praying with a prayer partner or several people, you should first ask for requests and then take turns praying for one another. Because of our busy schedules and fast-paced lifestyle, it may be impossible to meet at church for a prayer meeting during the day; however, most people have cell phones and can stay connected anywhere and anytime.

What if you called two people on a three-way phone call every day for prayer? In one week, you could pray with fourteen people. You may be saying, "I don't have the time to pray like that every day." What if you had prayer on the phone only once a week? You would have prayed with two more people than you would have otherwise.

A significant hindrance to effective prayer is praying with low expectations. After coming down from the Mount of Transfiguration, Jesus was approached by a man whose son was possessed by a demon. The disciples were unable to heal the boy, so the father approached Jesus for help saying, **"Lord, have mercy on my son, for he is an epileptic and he suffers terribly. For often he falls into the fire, and**

often into the water. And I brought him to your disciples, and they could not heal him" (Matthew 17:15-16). Jesus became indignant over His disciples who had access to the power of God but were unable to heal the man's son. After being questioned by Jesus, the father responded, **"I believe, help my unbelief!"** (Mark 9:24) Later that day, the disciples asked Jesus to explain the reason for their failure. Jesus connected the matter to an issue of unbelief by pointing to the disciples' "little faith."

Do you expect God to move when you pray or do you simply go through the motions? Scripture is clear about God acting according to His own will and purpose (Romans 8:28), but at the same time, He commands us to seek Him in prayer (Luke 11:9; Matthew 7:7). Remember the words of James, **"You do not have, because you do not ask"** (James 4:2). Keep in mind that prayer does more for the person making the request than merely obtaining the petition being presented. Some of my requests have been altered after long periods with God.

Start asking and expecting God to move.

SUGGESTED READING

E. M. Bounds, *The Classic Collection on Prayer* (Gainesville, FL: Bridge-Logos Publishers, 2001).

Andrew Murray, *With Christ in the School of Prayer* (Peabody, MA: Hendrickson Publishers, 2007).

Henry Blackaby and Norman Blackaby, *Experiencing Prayer with Jesus* (Colorado Springs, CO: Multnomah Books, 2006).

Donald Whitney, *Spiritual Disciplines for the Christian Life* (Colorado Springs, CO: NavPress, 1994).

Richard J. Foster, *Prayer: Finding the Heart's True Home* (Downers Grove, IL: InterVarsity Press, 1992).

4

Helping
Obeying the Word

—⟨⟩—

*"And what you have heard from me in
the presence of many witnesses entrust to
faithful men who will be able
to teach others also."*
2 Timothy 2:2

What does God desire?

B efore ascending into heaven, Jesus gave his
followers a command in Matthew 28:19, **"Go
therefore and make disciples."** This mandate is also

directed toward modern-day Christians to become

disciple-makers. In his book *The Great Omission*, Dallas Willard opens with an interesting illustration. He writes:

> If your neighbor is having trouble with his automobile, you might think he just got a lemon. And you might be right. But if you found that he was supplementing his gasoline with a quart of water now and then, you would not blame the car or its maker for it not running, or for running in fits and starts. You would say that the car was not built to work under the conditions imposed by the owner. And you would certainly advise him to put only the appropriate kind of fuel in the tank. After some restorative work perhaps the car would then run fine.[1]

The church has been providing new believers with the wrong fuel for growth. The problem is not with the Creator or the plan; the problem is with the lack of emphasis on discipleship by leaders of his movement, namely pastors. Bill Hull, a leading author in the area of discipleship, states, "I find it particularly puzzling that we struggle to put disciple-making at the center of ministry even though Jesus left us with the clear imperative to "make disciples."[2]

The term Christian is used three times in the Bible (Acts 11:26; 26:28; and 1 Peter 4:16). Only recently has the label "Christian" carried a positive meaning. According to *Harper's Bible Dictionary*, "Some have argued that the designation was at first a term of derision; others, that it simply denoted a group loyal to 'Christ.'"[3] It was a term given to followers of Christ by unbelievers. Jesus was not interested in making just "converts;" He was committed to making disciples. Interestingly, the word disciple is used 269 times in the New Testament and 238 times in the Gospels alone.

A disciple is a learner, an apprentice, or a student. Clearly, Jesus is interested in producing disciples, not just Christians. How many followers of Christ do you know that are disciples in the sense that Jesus intended? If a disciple is defined as a student or as a learner, can someone fall short in being a disciple if he or she stops learning? Let me ask the question another way. Can a person be a disciple without graduating from a seminary? Or, can a person who has been the pastor of a church for fifty years not be a disciple? Is that possible? The answer to all of the questions is yes. A life without learning is a life without discipleship.

Was Jesus interested in discipleship?

Archeologists have uncovered an inscription of the words "Pontius Pilate" on the side of an amphitheatre constructed by Herod that dates between 22-10 B.C. (According to Matthew 27, Pilate condemned Jesus to the cross at the request of the High Priest and elders to prevent the people from rioting). This theatre was the first of its kind. Built with granite columns, the magnificent structure provides seating for 3,500 to 4,000 people (for a photo of the theatre, see http://www.bibleplaces.com/caesarea.htm). Where is this theatre located? It was built on the seacoast in the town of Caesarea. Less than thirty miles from the birthplace of Christ, it is very likely that Jesus visited this town. Regardless, archeologists are certain that he at least knew of the structure. The reason for bringing this up is to prove a point about discipleship. If Jesus had been an American preacher, he would have sent his disciples into the region with a mission: Invite everyone to attend the Revival at Caesarea.

The local media would have advertised the event as, "The Greatest Sermon on Earth. The lame will walk, the blind will see, the deaf will hear, and the dead will rise. Ladies and gentlemen, boys and girls, kids of all ages, come and meet God in the flesh — Jesus the Christ." The disciples would have been sent through the town with flyers in hand and instructions to place them on every chariot and horse carriage they could find. It would have been billed as the biggest revival the world has ever seen. If Jesus had carried out ministry like many of our pastors today, He would have packed the place with people every night for months. Cards would have been signed, hands would have been raised, and people would have walked the aisles.

Conversely, Jesus was not an American pastor; he was a First Century Jewish Rabbi who believed in discipling twelve men.[4] There is no record of Jesus ever preaching at this amphitheatre, or for that matter, even visiting the city of Caesarea. Why? Not interested in drawing a massive audience, Jesus spent his life investing in twelve men. Yes, He spoke to large crowds on occasion (Matt. 14:13-21; 15:32-39), but, for the most part, he spent his life training a few men. If Jesus led the way for us, shouldn't we follow his lead?

Knowledge or knowing?

The goal of discipleship is not to merely gain knowledge about God but to know God. When we think of gaining knowledge, we think of filling our minds with as much information as possible. But filling our minds with information is not the same thing as knowing. There are many men and women who have read through the entire Bible multiple times and have attended church every Sunday, yet they are far from being disciples of Christ.

Knowledge alone does not equate to intimacy with God. When Jesus said, **"And you will know the truth, and the truth will set you free"** (John 8:32), He was not referring to information or "data." He was, however, thinking of *daat*. *Daat* is the Hebrew word for knowing and is used to describe the sexual oneness of a husband and wife. Genesis 4:1 uses the word: **"Adam *knew* Eve his wife, and she conceived and bore Cain."** The knowing that is the basis of discipleship involves more than reading the Bible, memorizing Scripture, and praying. It is intimately walking in communion with the Father. This intimate communion comes through living, loving, and spending time with God.

If knowing could be transmitted instantly, Jesus would have placed his hands on the apostles' heads and said, "know the truth." Instead, He said, you shall know the truth, implying that knowing is a process. The knowing that is involved in discipleship is the process of putting the principles of the Bible into practice in the walk of your everyday life.

What was the work Jesus was given to do?

Too many Christians have bought into the idea that Christianity is about reciting a prayer and professing a decision to receive Jesus in order to get into heaven. A.W. Tozer believed that "a notable heresy has come into being throughout evangelical

Christianity circles—the widely accepted concept that we humans can choose to accept Christ only because we need him as Savior and that we have the right to postpone our obedience to him as Lord as long as we want to…. Salvation apart from obedience is unknown in the sacred Scripture."[5] We are obedient to Christ when we follow his command to "make disciples."

Before Jesus went to the cross, he prayed for His disciples, not only for the twelve, but also for all those who would thereafter become His disciples. John records this prayer in chapter 17 of his Gospel. In His prayer, Jesus says, **"I glorified you on earth, having accomplished the work that you gave me to do"** (John 17:4). God gave Him a task to complete, and He finished it. The word accomplished means to carry something to completion or to bring to an end. The New King James Version translates verse 4 as, **"I have finished the work which You have given Me to do."**

What was the work Jesus was given to do? The context of the passage provides the answer. Many would argue that Jesus was talking about dying on the cross. This, however, cannot be true, for His prayer preceded the crucifixion, and He could not then have described His work as having been accomplished. The language of the prayer itself reveals that the work that Jesus was given to do was to train disciples.

Leroy Eims in his book *The Lost Art of Discipleship* states, "When you read the prayer carefully, you'll notice that He did not mention miracles or multitudes, but forty times He referred to the men whom God had given Him out of the world."[6] Jesus invested in people, not programs. Yes, He spoke to the multitudes, but He spent his life with twelve men. Before leaving this earth, it was no coincidence that Jesus commanded his disciples to follow his footsteps in making disciples: **"Go therefore and make**

disciples of all nations, baptizing them in the name of the Father and of the Son and of the Holy Spirit, teaching them to observe all that I have commanded you" (Matthew 28:19-20). The imperative command is not to go but to *make disciples.* How do you make disciples? Jesus tells us, **"teaching them to observe all that I have commanded you. "** In order to teach others what Jesus commanded, you must know His words yourself. It is important to get into the Word until the Word gets into you.

What needs to takes place in a discipleship group?

The goal for a discipleship group is to create an atmosphere for fellowship, encouragement, and accountability. This can be accomplished with a group of at least two but no more than five people. The meeting can take place at someone's home, at a restaurant, in a break room, or at church. An identifiable speaker is not needed since each participant will be responsible for sharing comments from his or her journal.

The group time should begin with a word of prayer. Then each person can recite the memory verse for the week. Open discussion of what was studied the previous week should take up the remainder of the meeting, with each member reading what he or she H.E.A.R.d from God. The group should be reminded that there are no wrong responses because the point is to H.E.A.R. from God and apply it to one's life.

When I started meeting with my first discipleship group, three of us attended the meeting each week with each letter of H.E.A.R. filled in, but one member of the group was hesitant to begin. Prior to committing to the discipleship group, his excuse for not reading the Word was, "It doesn't really speak to me." Seeing what God was doing through the others challenged him to start contributing to the group.

Soon thereafter, he would arrive saying, "Let me tell you what God spoke to me this week."

How important is obedience to you?

A disciple is someone who disciplines himself or herself to be obedient unto the Lord. Donald Whitney said:

> So many professing Christians are so spiritually undisciplined that they seem to have little fruit and power in their lives. I've seen men and women who discipline themselves for the purpose of excelling in their profession, but discipline themselves very little for the purpose of godliness. I've seen Christians who are faithful to the church of God, who frequently demonstrate genuine enthusiasm for the things of God, and who dearly love the Word of God, trivialize their effectiveness for the Kingdom of God through lack of discipline. Spiritually they are a mile wide and an inch deep. There are not deep, time-worn channels of communing discipline between them and God. They have dabbled in everything but disciplined themselves in nothing.[7]

We will give an account at the end of our lives. Are you willing to discipline yourself so that you are a disciple? Are you willing to be obedient and disciple others?

SUGGESTED READING

Bill Hull, *The Complete Book of Discipleship: On Being and Making Followers of Christ* (Colorado Springs, CO: NavPress, 2006).

Leroy Eims, *The Lost Art of Discipleship* (Grand Rapids, MI: Zondervan, 1978).

Greg Ogden, *Transforming Discipleship: Making a Few Disciples at a Time* (Downers Grove, IL: InterVarsity Press, 2003).

Christopher B. Adsit, *Personal Disciplemaking: A Step-by-Step Guide for Leading a Christian From New Birth to Maturity* (Orlando, FL: Campus Crusade for Christ, 1996).

Dallas Willard, *The Great Omission* (San Francisco, CA: HarperCollins Publications, 2006).

Win Arn and Charles Arn, The Master's Plan for Making Disciples: Every Christian an Effective Witness through an Enabling Church 2nd ed. (Grand Rapids, MI: Baker Books, 1982; 1998).

AFTERWORD

Established in 1958, the Queen's Baton Relay initiated the Commonwealth Games. Similar to the passing of the Olympic Torch, the Queen's baton is handed to a runner to begin the relay race. Unlike the Torch, this baton has a hand written note tucked inside. The race traditionally begins at Buckingham Palace in London, and it travels around the country before returning back to the Queen. In full view of the ensuing crowd, the Queen removes the note from the baton and reads it aloud to the people. A huge celebration begins, symbolizing the Opening Ceremony of the Commonwealth Games. The last relay took place in the 2006 Melbourne games in Australia. Spanning 112,000 miles and traveling through all 71 nations of the Commonwealth, it took a year and a day for the baton to return to the Queen.[1] That's a pretty impressive relay race, right?

Did you know that you are running in a relay race? As believers, we are not running in the Queen's Baton Relay, but we are running the race for the King of Kings. The author of Hebrews states, **"Therefore, since we are surrounded by so great a cloud of witnesses, let us also lay aside every weight, and sin which clings so closely, and *let us run with endurance the race that is set before us,* looking to Jesus, the founder and perfecter of our faith"** (Hebrews 12:1-2; emphasis added). Jesus passed the baton to His followers almost 2000 years ago, by saying, **"Go therefore and make disciples of all nations, baptizing them in the name of the Father and of the Son and of the Holy Spirit, teaching**

them to observe all that I have commanded you" (Matthew 28:19-20).

Before ascending into Heaven, Jesus passed the baton to his disciples, his loyal followers. The pages of Scripture detail the journey of this baton as it has passed from generation to generation. Some of the carriers of the baton have stories that are painted with struggles and failures, but certainly with restoration and triumph. Our recent pages of history continue the story of those who have been handed the baton and have faithfully carried the message of Jesus Christ. The intent is clear: Jesus wants His baton to be carried and passed along.

Look at your hands and see what you hold. Whether or not you feel worthy or ready, the baton has been passed to you. What are you going to do with it? Are you fumbling the handoff, or are you running with passion and conviction? Are you making disciples? Just as the Queen gave a baton to her messengers to take around the country, the King of Kings has given us a baton to take to the world. One day we will meet the King of the Universe face to face in order to give the baton back to the Him. What If Jesus' last words to his disciples were his first words to you and me when we meet him? What if the message in the baton reads, "Well done my good and faithful servant!" Don't be mistaken. Jesus will not lie on that day. He will not say "Well Done," if you have not DONE WELL. Take the baton, run the race, and pass it on.

ENDNOTES

Endnotes for the Introduction

[1]All Scripture references are from the ESV, unless otherwise stated.

Endnotes for Chapter 1

[1]To learn more about the Life Journal go to: www. lifejournal.cc.

[2]A. Berkeley Mickelsen, *Interpreting the Bible* (Grand Rapids, MI: Eerdmans Publishing, 1972), 113.

[3]Robert L. Sumner, *The Wonder of the Word of God,* [Internet] http://www.bible.org/illus.php?topic_id=158, Accessed 22 December 2008.

Endnotes for Chapter 2

[1]Jeffrey Douglass, *Living from Your Soul,* [Internet] http://books.google.com/books?id=u376gzdEfWcC, Accessed 21 December 2008.

[2]Dwight Pryor, *Hebrew Spirituality.* The Center for Judaic-Christian Studies, www.jcstudies.org. Audio message.

[3]Donald Whitney, *Spiritual Disciplines for the Christian Life* (Colorado Springs, CO: NavPress, 1994), 48.

[4]Thomas Watson, *Puritan Sermons,* vol. 2 (Wheaton, IL: Richard Owen Roberts, 1674; 1981), 62.

Endnotes for Chapter 3

[1]Andrew Murray, *With Christ in the School of Prayer* (Peabody, MA: Hendrickson Publishers, 2007), 118.

[2]Eugene Peterson, *Tell It Slant: A Conversation on the Language of Jesus in His Stories and Prayers* (Grand Rapids, MI: Eerdmans Publishing, 2008), 169.

Endnotes for Chapter 4

[1]Dallas Willard, *The Great Omission* (San Francisco, CA: HarperCollins Publications, 2006), xi.

[2]Bill Hull, *The Complete Book of Discipleship: On Being and Making Followers of Christ* (Colorado Springs, CO: NavPress, 2006), 24.

[3]P. J. Achtemeier, *Harper's Bible Dictionary* (San Francisco: Harper & Row, 1985), 163.

[4]Dwight Pryor, *Walk After Me* [audio teaching] The Center for Judaic Christian Studies, http://www. jcstudies.org, Accessed 25 January 2009.

[5]A. W. Tozer, *I Call It Heresy* (Harrisburg, PA: Christian Publications, 1974), 5.

[6]Leroy Eims, *The Lost Art of Discipleship* (Grand Rapids, MI: Zondervan, 1978), 28.

[7]Donald Whitney, *Spiritual Disciplines for the Christian Life* (Colorado Springs, CO: NavPress, 1994), 59.

Endnotes for Afterword

[1]The Commonwealth Games, [Internet] http:// www.thecgf.com/qbr, Accessed 21 January 2009.

Endnotes for Appendix 3

[1]The hand illustration was developed by the Navigators (www.navigators.org) and personalized by Tim LaFleur.

Endnotes for Appendix 5

[1]Jerry and Marilyn Fine, *One on One with God* (Enumclaw, WA: Winepress, 2003), 45-62.

APPENDIX 1[*]

H.E.A.R. Entry

Date: 1-21-09
Title: Meditation

H. (*Highlight*) "Think over what I say, for the Lord will give you understanding in everything."

2 Timothy 2:7

E. (*Explain*) Paul encouraged Timothy to ponder what he taught him. Casual thinking will not uncover deep doctrinal truths of the faith. Meditation leads to proper understanding.

A. (*Apply*) It is important for us to spend time meditating on the Word of the Lord. Memorization provides a way for me to saturate my mind with God's Word. Paul also told the church at Colossae to "Set your minds on things that are above, not on things that are on earth." (Colossians 3:1).

R. (*Respond*) God give me a hunger for Your word through the memorization of Scripture. Speak to me as I meditate on Your truths and precepts.

[*]**All of the appendixes can be downloaded from our website: www.awordfromhisword.org.**

APPENDIX 2

Scripture Memory Cards

All authority in heaven and on earth has been given to me. Go therefore and make disciples of all nations, baptizing them in the name of the Father and of the Son and of the Holy Spirit, teaching them to observe all that I have commanded you. And behold, I am with you always, to the end of the age.

All Scripture is breathed out by God and profitable for teaching, for reproof, for correction, and for training in righteousness, that the man of God may be competent, equipped for every good work.

But in your hearts honor Christ the Lord as holy, always being prepared to make a defense to anyone who asks you for a reason for the hope that is in you; yet do it with gentleness and respect.

And I am sure of this, that he who began a good work in you will bring it to completion at the day of Jesus Christ.

For by grace you have been saved through faith. And this is not your own doing; it is the gift of God, not a result of works, so that no one may boast.

Therefore, if anyone is in Christ, he is a new creation. The old has passed away; behold, the new has come.

I have been crucified with Christ. It is no longer I who live, but Christ who lives in me. And the life I now live in the flesh I live by faith in the Son of God, who loved me and gave himself for me.

No temptation has overtaken you that is not common to man. God is faithful, and he will not let you be tempted beyond your ability, but with the temptation he will also provide the way of escape, that you may be able to endure it.

I appeal to you therefore, brothers, by the mercies of God, to present your bodies as a living sacrifice, holy and acceptable to God, which is your spiritual worship. Do not be conformed to this world, but be transformed by the renewal of your mind, that by testing you may discern what is the will of God, what is good and acceptable and perfect.

If anyone would come after me, let him deny himself and take up his cross daily and follow me.

For God so loved the world, that he gave his only Son, that whoever believes in him should not perish, but have eternal life.

Trust in the Lord with all your heart, and do not lean on your own understanding. In all your ways acknowledge him, and he will make straight your paths.

I have stored up your word in my heart, that I might no sin against you.

Blessed is the man who walks not in the counsel of the wicked, nor stands in the way of sinners, nor sits in the seat of scoffers; but his delight is in the law of the Lord, and on his law he mediates day and night.

For even the Son of Man came not to be served but to serve, and to give his life as a ransom for many.

Scripture Memory Cards (verses are from left to right). These verses should be written on the back of each of the above cards.

Matthew 28:18-20
2 Timothy 3:16-17
1 Peter 3:15
Philippians 1:6
Ephesians 2:8-9
2 Corinthians 5:17
Galatians 2:20
1 Corinthians 10:13
Romans 12:1-2
Luke 9:23
John 3:16
Proverbs 3:5, 6
Psalm 119:11
Psalm 1: 1-2
Mark 10:45

APPENDIX 3

Saturating Your Life with the Word of God[1]

APPENDIX 4

Prayer Log

Date Asked	Prayer Request	Date Answered

Reading Plan

JANUARY[1]

"And beginning with Moses and with all the prophets,
He explained to them all the things concerning
Himself in all the Scriptures."
(Luke 24:27)

1	☐ Gen. 1:1-2:3	☐ Job 1:1-2:10	☐ Matt. 1
2	☐ Gen. 2:4-25	☐ Job 2:11-3:26	☐ Matt. 2
3	☐ Gen. 3	☐ Job 4,5	☐ Matt. 3
4	☐ Gen. 4, 5	☐ Job 6,7	☐ Matt. 4
5	☐ Gen 6:1-7:10	☐ Job 8	☐ Matt. 5:1-20
6	☐ Gen. 7:11-8:19	☐ Job 9, 10	☐ Matt. 5:21-48
7	☐ Gen. 8:20-9:29	☐ Job 11, 12	☐ Matt. 6:1-18
8	☐ Gen. 10:1-11:26	☐ Job 13, 14	☐ Matt. 6:19-7:6
9	☐ Gen 11:27-12:10	☐ Job 15	☐ Matt. 7:7-29
10	☐ Gen. 13,14	☐ Job 16,17	☐ Matt. 8:1-27
11	☐ Gen. 15,16	☐ Job 18,19	☐ Matt. 8:28-9:17
12	☐ Gen. 17	☐ Job 20	☐ Matt. 9:18-38
13	☐ Gen. 18	☐ Job 21	☐ Matt. 10:1-25
14	☐ Gen. 19	☐ Job 22	☐ Matt. 10:26-11:1
15	☐ Gen. 20,21	☐ Job 23,24	☐ Matt. 11:2-30
16	☐ Gen. 22	☐ Job 25-27	☐ Matt.12:1-21
17	☐ Gen. 23	☐ Job 28	☐ Matt. 12:22-50
18	☐ Gen. 24	☐ Job 29,30	☐ Matt. 13:1-23
19	☐ Gen. 25	☐ Job 31	☐ Matt.13:24-43
20	☐ Gen. 26	☐ Job 32,33	☐ Matt. 13:44-14:13
21	☐ Gen. 27	☐ Job 34,35	☐ Matt.14:14-36
22	☐ Gen. 28	☐ Job 36,37	☐ Matt. 15:1-28

23	☐ Gen. 29	☐ Job 38,39	☐ Matt. 15:29-16:12
24	☐ Gen. 30	☐ Job 40,41	☐ Matt. 16:13-17:13
25	☐ Gen. 31	☐ Job 42	☐ Matt. 17:14-18:14
26	☐ Gen. 32:1-33:16	☐ Psalm 1-3	☐ Matt. 18:15-35
27	☐ Gen. 33:17-34:31	☐ Psalm 4-6	☐ Matt. 19:1-15
28	☐ Gen. 35	☐ Psalm 7,8	☐ Matt. 19:16-20:16
29	☐ Gen. 36	☐ Psalm 9,10	☐ Matt.20:17-34
30	☐ Gen. 37	☐ Psalm 11-14	☐ Matt.21:1-32
31	☐ Gen. 38	☐ Psalm 15,16	☐ Matt. 21:33-22:14

FEBRUARY

"The law of the Lord is perfect, restoring the soul:
the testimony of the Lord is sure, making wise the simple."
(Psalm 19:7)

1	☐ Gen. 39	☐ Psalm 17	☐ Matt. 22:15-46
2	☐ Gen. 40	☐ Psalm 18:1-29	☐ Matt. 23
3	☐ Gen. 41:1-49	☐ Psalm 18:30-50	☐ Matt. 24:1-28
4	☐ Gen. 41:50-42:38	☐ Psalm 19	☐ Matt. 24:29-51
5	☐ Gen. 43	☐ Psalm 20,21	☐ Matt. 25:1-30
6	☐ Gen. 44	☐ Psalm 22	☐ Matt. 25:31-26:2
7	☐ Gen. 45	☐ Psalm 23,24	☐ Matt.26:3-30
8	☐ Gen. 46:1-47:26	☐ Psalm 25	☐ Matt. 26:31-57
9	☐ Gen. 47:27-48:22	☐ Psalm 26,27	☐ Matt. 26:58-75
10	☐ Gen. 49	☐ Psalm 28,29	☐ Matt. 27:1-26
11	☐ Gen. 50	☐ Psalm 30	☐ Matt. 27:27-44
12	☐ Ex. 1:1-2:22	☐ Psalm 31	☐ Matt. 27:45-68
13	☐ Ex. 2:23-3:22	☐ Psalm 32,33	☐ Matt. 28
14	☐ Ex. 4	☐ Psalm 34	☐ Acts 1
15	☐ Ex. 5:1-6:12	☐ Psalm 35,36	☐ Acts 2:1-21
16	☐ Ex. 6:13-7:25	☐ Psalm 37	☐ Acts 2:22-47
17	☐ Ex. 8	☐ Psalm 38,39	☐ Acts 3
18	☐ Ex. 9	☐ Psalm 40,41	☐ Acts 4:1-31
19	☐ Ex. 10	☐ Psalm 42,43	☐ Acts 4:32-5:11
20	☐ Ex. 11:1-12:20	☐ Psalm 44	☐ Acts 5:12-42
21	☐ Ex. 12:21-51	☐ Psalm 45,46	☐ Acts 6
22	☐ Ex. 13:1-14:4	☐ Psalm 47,48	☐ Acts 7:1-29
23	☐ Ex. 14:5-31	☐ Psalm 49,50	☐ Acts 7:30-8:4
24	☐ Ex. 15	☐ Psalm 51	☐ Acts 8:5-40
25	☐ Ex. 16	☐ Psalm 52,53, 54	☐ Acts 9:1-31
26	☐ Ex. 17	☐ Psalm 55	☐ Acts 9:32-43
27	☐ Ex. 18	☐ Psalm 56,57	☐ Acts 10:1-23
28	☐ Ex. 19	☐ Psalm 58, 59	☐ Acts 10:24-48

MARCH

"How can a young man keep his way pure?
By keeping it according to Thy word."
(Psalm 119:9)

1	☐ Ex. 20	☐ Psalm 60,61	☐ Acts 11:1-18
2	☐ Ex. 21	☐ Psalm 62,63	☐ Acts 11:19-30
3	☐ Ex. 22:1-23:9	☐ Psalm 64,65	☐ Acts 12
4	☐ Ex. 23:10-33	☐ Psalm 66,67	☐ Acts 13:1-25
5	☐ Ex. 24	☐ Psalm 68	☐ Acts 13:26-52
6	☐ Ex. 25	☐ Psalm 69	☐ Acts 14
7	☐ Ex. 26:1-30	☐ Psalm 70,71	☐ Acts 15:1-21
8	☐ Ex. 26:31-27:19	☐ Psalm 72	☐ Acts 15:22-35
9	☐ Ex. 27:20-28:14	☐ Psalm 73	☐ Acts 15:36-16:15
10	☐ Ex. 28:15-43	☐ Psalm 74,75	☐ Acts 16:16-40
11	☐ Ex. 29:1-37	☐ Psalm 76,77	☐ Acts 17:1-15
12	☐ Ex. 29:38-30:10	☐ Psalm 78:1-31	☐ Acts 17:16-34
13	☐ Ex. 30:11-38	☐ Psalm 78:32-72	☐ Acts 18:1-22
14	☐ Ex. 31	☐ Psalm 79,80	☐ Acts 18:1-22
15	☐ Ex. 32	☐ Psalm 81,82	☐ Acts 19:1-41
16	☐ Ex. 33:1-34:3	☐ Psalm 83,84	☐ Acts 20:1-16
17	☐ Ex. 34:4-35	☐ Psalm 85,86	☐ Acts 20:17-38
18	☐ Ex. 35	☐ Psalm 87,88	☐ Acts 21:1-16
19	☐ Ex. 36	☐ Psalm 89:1-18	☐ Acts 21:17-40
20	☐ Ex. 37	☐ Psalm 89:19-52	☐ Acts 22:1-21
21	☐ Ex. 38	☐ Psalm 90,91	☐ Acts 22:22-23:11
22	☐ Ex. 39	☐ Psalm 92,93	☐ Acts 23:12-35
23	☐ Ex. 40	☐ Psalm 95,95	☐ Acts 24
24	☐ Lev. 1	☐ Psalm 96,97, 98	☐ Acts 25:1-22
25	☐ Lev. 2	☐ Psalm 99, 100, 101	☐ Acts 25:23-26:11
26	☐ Lev. 3	☐ Psalm 102	☐ Acts 26:12-32
27	☐ Lev. 4:1-26	☐ Psalm 103	☐ Acts 27:1-26
28	☐ Lev. 4:27-5:13	☐ Psalm 104	☐ Acts 27:27-28:10
29	☐ Lev. 5:14-6:7	☐ Psalm 105	☐ Acts 28:11-31

30	☐ Lev. 6:8-7:10	☐ Psalm 106	☐ Mark 1:1-20
31	☐ Lev. 7:11-38	☐ Psalm 107	☐ Mark 1:21-45

APRIL

"But these have been written that you may believe that Jesus
is the Christ, the Son of God; and that believing you may have
life in His name."
(John 20:31)

1	☐ Lev. 8	☐ Psalm 108	☐ Mark 2:1-22
2	☐ Lev. 9	☐ Psalm 109	☐ Mark 2:23-3:12
3	☐ Lev. 10	☐ Psalm 110, 111	☐ Mark 3:13-35
4	☐ Lev. 11	☐ Psalm 112, 113, 114	☐ Mark 4:1-20
5	☐ Lev. 12:1-13:23	☐ Psalm 115, 116	☐ Mark 4:21-41
6	☐ Lev. 13:24-59	☐ Psalm 117, 118	☐ Mark 5:1-20
7	☐ Lev. 14:1-32	☐ Psalm 119:1-40	☐ Mark 5:21-43
8	☐ Lev. 14:33-57	☐ Psalm 119:41-72	☐ Mark 6:1-29
9	☐ Lev. 15	☐ Psalm 119:73-112	☐ Mark 6:30-56
10	☐ Lev. 16	☐ Psalm119:113-144	☐ Mark 7:1-23
11	☐ Lev. 17,18	☐ Psalm119:145-176	☐ Mark 7:24-8:10
12	☐ Lev. 19,20	☐ Psalm 120-123	☐ Mark 8:11-26
13	☐ Lev. 21	☐ Psalm 124-127	☐ Mark 8:27-9:13
14	☐ Lev. 22	☐ Psalm 128-131	☐ Mark 9:14-32
15	☐ Lev. 23:1-22	☐ Psalm 132, 133	☐ Mark 9:33-50
16	☐ Lev. 23:23-44	☐ Psalm 134,135	☐ Mark 10:1-31
17	☐ Lev. 24	☐ Psalm 136, 137	☐ Mark 10:32-52
18	☐ Lev. 25	☐ Psalm 138,139	☐ Mark 11:1-26
19	☐ Lev. 26	☐ Psalm 140, 141	☐ Mark 11:27-12:17
20	☐ Lev. 27	☐ Psalm 142, 143	☐ Mark 12:18-44
21	☐ Num. 1	☐ Psalm 144, 145	☐ Mark 13
22	☐ Num. 2	☐ Psalm 146, 147	☐ Mark 14:1-26
23	☐ Num. 3	☐ Psalm 148-150	☐ Mark 14:27-52
24	☐ Num. 4	☐ Prov. 1	☐ Mark 14:53-72

25	☐ Num. 5	☐ Prov. 2	☐ Mark 15:1-23
26	☐ Num. 6	☐ Prov. 3	☐ Mark 5:24-47
27	☐ Num. 7	☐ Prov. 4	☐ Mark 16
28	☐ Num. 8	☐ Prov. 5:1-6:19	☐ 1 Pet. 1:1-12
29	☐ Num. 9:1-10:10	☐ Prov. 6:20-7:27	☐ 1 Pet. 1:13-2:10
30	☐ Num. 10:11-11:3	☐ Prov. 8	☐ 1 Pet. 2:11-3:7

MAY

"Like newborn babies, long for the pure milk of the word,
that by it you may grow in respect to salvation."
(1 Peter 2:2)

1	☐ Num. 11:4-35	☐ Prov. 9	☐ 1 Pet. 3:8-22
2	☐ Num. 12,13	☐ Prov. 10	☐ 1 Pet. 4
3	☐ Num. 14	☐ Prov. 11	☐ 1 Pet. 5
4	☐ Num. 15	☐ Prov. 12	☐ 2 Pet. 1
5	☐ Num. 16:1-40	☐ Prov. 13	☐ 2 Pet. 2
6	☐ Num. 16:41-17:13	☐ Prov. 14	☐ 2 Pet. 3
7	☐ Num. 18	☐ Prov. 15	☐ James 1
8	☐ Num. 19	☐ Prov. 16	☐ James 2
9	☐ Num. 20	☐ Prov. 17	☐ James 3
10	☐ Num. 21	☐ Prov. 18	☐ James 4
11	☐ Num. 22:1-38	☐ Prov. 19	☐ James 5
12	☐ Num 22:39-23:26	☐ Prov. 20:1-21:11	☐ Jude
13	☐ Num. 23:27-24:25	☐ Prov. 21:12-22:16	☐ Luke 1:1-25
14	☐ Num. 25:1-26:51	☐ Prov. 22:17-23:11	☐ Luke 1:26-56
15	☐ Num. 26:52-27:23	☐ Prov. 23:12-35	☐ Luke 1:57-80
16	☐ Num. 28	☐ Prov. 24	☐ Luke 2:1-21
17	☐ Num. 29	☐ Prov. 25:1-26:12	☐ Luke 2:22-52
18	☐ Num. 30,31	☐ Prov. 26:13-27:27	☐ Luke 3
19	☐ Num. 32	☐ Prov. 28	☐ Luke 4:1-15
20	☐ Num. 33	☐ Prov. 29	☐ Luke 4:16-44
21	☐ Num. 34:1-35:8	☐ Prov. 30	☐ Luke 5:1-16
22	☐ Num. 35:9	☐ Prov. 31	☐ Luke 5:17-39
23	☐ Deut. 1	☐ Eccl. 1:1-2:10	☐ Luke 6:1-19
24	☐ Deut. 2	☐ Eccl. 2:11-3:15	☐ Luke 6:20-49
25	☐ Deut. 3	☐ Eccl. 3:16-4:16	☐ Luke 7:1-29
26	☐ Deut. 4	☐ Eccl. 5, 6	☐ Luke 7:30-50
27	☐ Deut. 5	☐ Eccl. 7	☐ Luke 8:1-21
28	☐ Deut. 6:1-7:10	☐ Eccl. 8:1-9:10	☐ Luke 8:22-39

29	☐ Deut. 7:11-8:20	☐ Eccl. 9:11-10:20	☐ Luke 8:40-56
30	☐ Deut. 9:1-10:11	☐ Eccl. 11,12	☐ Luke 9:1-17
31	☐ Deut. 10:12-11:32	☐ Song. 1:1-2:7	☐ Luke 9:18-36

JUNE

"The gospel of God, which He promised beforehand
through His prophets in the holy Scriptures."
(Romans 1:1,2)

1	☐ Deut. 12	☐ Song. 2:8-3:5	☐ Luke 9:37-62
2	☐ Deut. 13:1-14:21	☐ Song. 3:6-5:1	☐ Luke 10:1-24
3	☐ Deut. 14:22-15:23	☐ Song. 5:2-6:9	☐ Luke 10:25-42
4	☐ Deut. 16	☐ Song. 6:10-8:14	☐ Luke 11:1-13
5	☐ Deut. 17:1-18:8	☐ Obadiah	☐ Luke 11:14-36
6	☐ Deut. 18:9-19:21	☐ Joel 1	☐ Luke 11:37-54
7	☐ Deut. 20,21	☐ Joel 2	☐ Luke 12:1-21
8	☐ Deut. 22:1-23:8	☐ Joel 3	☐ Luke 12:22-40
9	☐ Deut. 23:9-24:22	☐ Jonah 1,2	☐ Luke 12:41-59
10	☐ Deut. 25:1-26:15	☐ Jonah 3,4	☐ Luke 13:1-21
11	☐ Deut. 26:16-27:26		☐ Luke 13:22-35
12	☐ Deut. 28:1-37		☐ Luke 14:1-24
13	☐ Deut. 28:38-68	☐ Amos 1,2	☐ Luke 14:25-15:10
14	☐ Deut. 29	☐ Amos 3,4	☐ Luke 15:11-32
15	☐ Deut. 30:1-31:13	☐ Amos 5,6	☐ Luke 16
16	☐ Deut. 31:14-32:14	☐ Hosea 1:1-2:1	☐ Luke 17:1-19
17	☐ Deut. 32:15-52	☐ Hosea 2:2-3:5	☐ Luke 17:20-18:14
18	☐ Deut 33	☐ Hosea 4:1-6:3	☐ Luke 18:15-43
19	☐ Deut. 34	☐ Hosea 6:4-7:16	☐ Luke 19:1-28
20	☐ Joshua 1	☐ Hosea 8,9	☐ Luke 19:29-48
21	☐ Joshua 2	☐ Hosea 10:1 -11:11	☐ Luke 20:1-19
22	☐ Joshua 3	☐ Hosea 11:12 -14:9	☐ Luke 20:21-21:4
23	☐ Joshua 4:1-5:12	☐ Isa. 1	☐ Luke 21:5-38
24	☐ Joshua 5:13-6:27	☐ Isa. 2	☐ Luke 22:1-30
25	☐ Joshua 7	☐ Isa. 3,4	☐ Luke 22:31-53
26	☐ Joshua 8	☐ Isa. 5	☐ Luke 22:54-23:12
27	☐ Joshua 9	☐ Isa. 6	☐ Luke 23:13-46

28	☐ Joshua 10	☐ Isa. 7:1-8:4	☐ Luke 23:47-24:12
29	☐ Joshua 11, 12	☐ Isa. 8:5-9:7	☐ Luke 24:13-53
30	☐ Joshua 13	☐ Isa. 9:8-10:5	☐ 1 Thess. 1

JULY

"All Scripture is inspired by God and profitable for teaching,
for reproof, for corrections, for training in righteousness."
(2 Timothy 3:16)

1	☐ Joshua 14, 15	☐ Isa. 10:6-34	☐ 1 Thess. 2:1-16
2	☐ Joshua 16, 17	☐ Isa. 11, 12	☐ 1 Thess. 2:17-3:13
3	☐ Joshua 18, 19	☐ Isa. 13	☐ 1 Thess. 4
4	☐ Joshua 20, 21	☐ Isa. 14	☐ 1 Thess. 5
5	☐ Joshua 22	☐ Isa. 15, 16	☐ 2 Thess. 1
6	☐ Joshua 23	☐ Isa. 17, 18	☐ 2 Thess. 2
7	☐ Joshua 24	☐ Isa. 19, 20	☐ 2 Thess. 3
8	☐ Judges 1:1-2:5	☐ Isa. 21:1-22:14	☐ 1 Cor. 1
9	☐ Judges 2:6-3:4	☐ Isa. 22:15-23:18	☐ 1 Cor. 2
10	☐ Judges 3:5-31	☐ Isa. 24	☐ 1 Cor. 3
11	☐ Judges 4	☐ Isa. 25	☐ 1 Cor. 4
12	☐ Judges 5	☐ Isa. 26	☐ 1 Cor. 5
13	☐ Judges 6	☐ Isa. 27	☐ 1 Cor. 6
14	☐ Judges 7	☐ Isa. 28	☐ 1 Cor. 7
15	☐ Judges 8	☐ Isa. 29	☐ 1 Cor. 8
16	☐ Judges 9:1-10:5	☐ Isa. 30	☐ 1 Cor. 9:1-23
17	☐ Judges 10:6-11:28	☐ Isa. 31, 32	☐ 1 Cor. 9:24-10:14
18	☐ Judges 11:29-12:15	☐ Isa. 33	☐ 1 Cor. 10:15-11:1
19	☐ Judges 13	☐ Isa. 34, 35	☐ 1 Cor. 11:2-34
20	☐ Judges 14, 15	☐ Isa. 36:1-37:7	☐ 1 Cor. 12
21	☐ Judges 16	☐ Isa. 37:8-38	☐ 1 Cor. 13
22	☐ Judges 17, 18	☐ Isa. 38, 39	☐ 1 Cor. 14
23	☐ Judges 19	☐ Isa. 40	☐ 1 Cor. 15:1-34
24	☐ Judges 20	☐ Isa. 41:1-20	☐ 1 Cor. 15:35-58
25	☐ Judges 21	☐ Isa. 41:21-42:21	☐ 1 Cor. 16
26	☐ Ruth 1	☐ Isa. 42:22-43:10	☐ 2 Cor. 1
27	☐ Ruth 2	☐ Isa. 43:11-44:5	☐ 2 Cor. 2

28 ☐ Ruth 3, 4	☐ Isa. 44:6-23	☐ 2 Cor. 3:1-4:6
29 ☐ 1 Sam. 1	☐ Isa. 44:24-45:8	☐ 2 Cor. 4:7-5:10
30 ☐ 1 Sam. 2	☐ Isa. 45:9-25	☐ 2 Cor. 5:11-6:10
31 ☐ 1 Sam. 3	☐ Isa. 46	☐ 2 Cor. 6:11-7:16

AUGUST

"But know this first of all, that no prophecy of Scripture is a matter of one's own interpretation, for no prophecy was ever made by an act of human will, but men moved by the Holy Spirit spoke from God."
(2 Peter 1:20, 21)

1	☐ 1 Sam. 4, 5	☐ Isa. 47	☐ 2 Cor. 8
2	☐ 1 Sam 6, 7	☐ Isa. 48	☐ 2 Cor. 9
3	☐ 1 Sam 8:1-9:14	☐ Isa. 49	☐ 2 Cor. 10
4	☐ 1 Sam. 9:15 -10:27	☐ Isa. 50:1-51:8	☐ 2 Cor. 11
5	☐ 1 Sam. 11, 12	☐ Isa. 51:9-23	☐ 2 Cor. 12:1-13
6	☐ 1 Sam. 13	☐ Isa. 52:1-12	☐ 2 Cor. 12:14-13:14
7	☐ 1 Sam. 14	☐ Isa. 52:13-53:12	☐ Rom. 1:1-16
8	☐ 1 Sam. 15	☐ Isa. 54	☐ Rom. 1:17-32
9	☐ 1 Sam. 16	☐ Isa. 55:1-56:8	☐ Rom. 2
10	☐ 1 Sam. 17:1-31	☐ Isa. 56:9-57:21	☐ Rom. 3
11	☐ 1 Sam. 17:32-58	☐ Isa. 58	☐ Rom. 4:1-22
12	☐ 1 Sam. 18:1-19:7	☐ Isa. 59	☐ Rom. 4:23-5:11
13	☐ 1 Sam.19:8-20:42	☐ Isa. 60	☐ Rom. 5:12-21
14	☐ 1 Sam. 21, 22	☐ Isa. 61	☐ Rom. 6:1-14
15	☐ 1 Sam. 23, 24	☐ Isa. 62:1-63:14	☐ Rom. 6:15-7:6
16	☐ 1 Sam. 25	☐ Isa. 63:15-64:12	☐ Rom. 7:7-25
17	☐ 1 Sam. 26, 27	☐ Isa. 65	☐ Rom. 8:1-17
18	☐ 1 Sam. 28, 29	☐ Isa. 66	☐ Rom. 8:18-39
19	☐ 1 Sam. 30, 31	☐ Micah 1, 2	☐ Rom. 9:1-29
20	☐ 2 Sam. 1	☐ Micah 3:1-4:8	☐ Rom. 9:30-10:21
21	☐ 2 Sam. 2	☐ Micah 4:9-5:15	☐ Rom. 11:1-15
22	☐ 2 Sam. 3	☐ Micah 6	☐ Rom. 11:16-36
23	☐ 2 Sam. 4, 5	☐ Micah 7	☐ Rom. 12
24	☐ 2 Sam. 6	☐ Nahum 1	☐ Rom. 13
25	☐ 2 Sam. 7	☐ Nahum 2, 3	☐ Rom. 14:1-18
26	☐ 2 Sam. 8,9	☐ Hab. 1	☐ Rom. 14:19-15:13

27	☐ 2 Sam. 10, 11	☐ Hab. 2	☐ Rom. 15:14-33
28	☐ 2 Sam. 12	☐ Hab. 3	☐ Rom. 16
29	☐ 2 Sam. 13	☐ Zeph. 1	☐ Gal. 1
30	☐ 2 Sam. 14	☐ Zeph. 2	☐ Gal. 2
31	☐ 2 Sam. 15	☐ Zeph. 3	☐ Gal. 3:1-14

SEPTEMBER

"The Spirit of the Lord spoke by me,
and His word was on my tongue."
(2 Samuel 23:2)

1	☐ 2 Sam. 16, 17	☐ Jer. 1	☐ Gal. 3:15-29
2	☐ 2 Sam. 18:1-19:8	☐ Jer. 2	☐ Gal. 4:1-20
3	☐ 2 Sam. 19:9-43	☐ Jer. 3:1-4:2	☐ Gal. 4:21-5:9
4	☐ 2 Sam. 20	☐ Jer. 4:3-31	☐ Gal. 5:10-26
5	☐ 2 Sam. 21	☐ Jer. 5	☐ Gal. 6
6	☐ 2 Sam. 22	☐ Jer. 6	☐ Eph. 1:1-14
7	☐ 2 Sam. 23	☐ Jer. 7	☐ Eph. 1:15-2:10
8	☐ 2 Sam. 24	☐ Jer. 8	☐ Eph. 2:11-22
9	☐ 1 Kings 1	☐ Jer. 9	☐ Eph. 3
10	☐ 1 Kings 2	☐ Jer. 10	☐ Eph. 4:1-16
11	☐ 1 Kings 3	☐ Jer. 11	☐ Eph. 4:17-32
12	☐ 1 Kings 4, 5	☐ Jer. 12	☐ Eph. 5:1-21
13	☐ 1 Kings 6	☐ Jer. 13	☐ Eph. 5:22-6:9
14	☐ 1 Kings 7	☐ Jer. 14	☐ Eph. 6:10-24
15	☐ 1 Kings 8:1-30	☐ Jer. 15	☐ Phil. 1:1-20
16	☐ 1 Kings 8:31-66	☐ Jer. 16	☐ Phil 1:21-2:11
17	☐ 1 Kings 9	☐ Jer. 17	☐ Phil. 2:12-30
18	☐ 1 Kings 10	☐ Jer. 18	☐ Phil. 3:1-4:1
19	☐ 1 Kings 11	☐ Jer. 19, 20	☐ Phil. 4:2-23
20	☐ 1 Kings 12:1-24	☐ Jer. 22	☐ Col. 1:1-20
21	☐ 1 Kings 12:25 -13:32	☐ Jer. 23	☐ Col. 1:21-2:7
22	☐ 1 Kings 13:33 -14:31	☐ Jer. 25	☐ Col. 2:8-3:4
23	☐ 1 Kings 15:1-32	☐ Jer. 26	☐ Col. 3:5-4:1
24	☐ 1 Kings 15:33 -16:34	☐ Jer. 35	☐ Col. 4:2-18
25	☐ 1 Kings 17	☐ Jer. 36, 45	☐ Philemon
26	☐ 1 Kings 18	☐ Jer. 46, 47	☐ Heb. 1
27	☐ 1 Kings 19	☐ Jer. 48	☐ Heb. 2
28	☐ 1 Kings 20	☐ Jer. 49	☐ Heb. 3
29	☐ 1 Kings 21	☐ Jer. 50	☐ Heb. 4:1-13
30	☐ 1 Kings 22	☐ Jer. 51:1-24	☐ Heb. 4:14-5:10

OCTOBER
"The Scripture had to be fulfilled, which the Holy Spirit
foretold by the mouth of David concerning."
(Acts 1:16)

1	☐ 2 Kings 1	☐ Jer. 51:25-64	☐ Heb. 5:11-6:20
2	☐ 2 Kings 2	☐ Jer. 24, 29	☐ Heb. 7
3	☐ 2 Kings 3	☐ Jer. 30	☐ Heb. 8
4	☐ 2 Kings 4	☐ Jer. 31	☐ Heb. 9:1-14
5	☐ 2 Kings 5	☐ Jer. 27, 28	☐ Heb. 9:15-28
6	☐ 2 Kings 6:1-23	☐ Jer. 21, 34	☐ Heb. 10:1-18
7	☐ 2 Kings 6:24-7:20	☐ Jer. 37	☐ Heb. 10:19-39
8	☐ 2 Kings 8	☐ Jer. 32:1-25	☐ Heb. 11:1-16
9	☐ 2 Kings 9	☐ Jer. 32:26-44	☐ Heb. 11:17-40
10	☐ 2 Kings 10	☐ Jer. 33	☐ Heb. 12:1-17
11	☐ 2 Kings 11, 12	☐ Jer. 38	☐ Heb. 12:18-13:6
12	☐ 2 Kings 13:1 -14:22	☐ Jer. 39	☐ Heb. 13:7-25
13	☐ 2 Kings 14:23 -15:31	☐ Jer. 40	☐ Titus 1:1-2:28
14	☐ 2 Kings 15:32 -16:20	☐ Jer. 41	☐ Titus 2:9-3:15
15	☐ 2 Kings 17	☐ Jer. 42, 43	☐ 1 Tim. 1
16	☐ 2 Kings 18	☐ Jer. 44	☐ 1 Tim. 2
17	☐ 2 Kings 19	☐ Jer. 52	☐ 1 Tim. 3
18	☐ 2 Kings 20:1 -21:18	☐ Lam. 1	☐ 1 Tim. 4
19	☐ 2 Kings 21:19 -22:20	☐ Lam. 2	☐ 1 Tim. 5
20	☐ 2 Kings 23	☐ Lam. 3	☐ 1 Tim. 6
21	☐ 2 Kings 24	☐ Lam. 4, 5	☐ 2 Tim. 1
22	☐ 2 Kings 25	☐ Ezek. 1	☐ 2 Tim. 2
23	☐ 1 Chron. 1	☐ Ezek. 2:1-3:15	☐ 2 Tim. 3
24	☐ 1 Chron. 2	☐ Ezek. 3:16-4:17	☐ 2 Tim. 4
25	☐ 1 Chron. 3:1-4:23	☐ Ezek. 5, 6	☐ John 1:1-18
26	☐ 1 Chron. 4:24 -5:26	☐ Ezek. 7	☐ John 1:19-51

27	☐ 1 Chron. 6	☐ Ezek. 8, 9	☐ John 2:1-22
28	☐ 1 Chron. 7	☐ Ezek. 10	☐ John 2:23-3:21
29	☐ 1 Chron. 8, 9	☐ Ezek. 11	☐ John 3:22-36
30	☐ 1 Chron 10, 11	☐ Ezek. 12	☐ John 4:1-30
31	☐ 1 Chron. 12	☐ Ezek. 13	☐ John 4:31-54

NOVEMBER

"But the things which God announced beforehand by the mouth of all the prophets, that His Christ should suffer, He has thus fulfilled."

(Acts 3:18)

1	☐ 1 Chron. 13, 14	☐ Ezek. 14, 15	☐ John 5:1-23
2	☐ 1 Chron. 15	☐ Ezek. 16:1-34	☐ John 5:24-47
3	☐ 1 Chron. 16	☐ Ezek. 16:35-63	☐ John 6:1-21
4	☐ 1 Chron. 17, 18	☐ Ezek. 17	☐ John 6:22-40
5	☐ 1 Chron. 19, 20	☐ Ezek. 18, 19	☐ John 6:41-7:1
6	☐ 1 Chron. 21	☐ Ezek. 20:1-44	☐ John 7:2-30
7	☐ 1 Chron. 22, 23	☐ Ezek. 20:45 -21:32	☐ John 7:31-8:11
8	☐ 1 Chron. 24, 25	☐ Ezek. 22	☐ John 8:12-30
9	☐ 1 Chron. 26, 27	☐ Ezek. 23	☐ John 8:31-59
10	☐ 1 Chron. 28	☐ Ezek. 24, 25	☐ John 9:1-17
11	☐ 1 Chron. 29	☐ Ezek. 26	☐ John 9:18-38
12	☐ 2 Chron. 1, 2	☐ Ezek. 27	☐ John 9:39-10:18
13	☐ 2 Chron. 3, 4	☐ Ezek. 28	☐ John 10:19-42
14	☐ 2 Chron. 5:1-6:11	☐ Ezek. 29:1 -30:19	☐ John 11:1-27
15	☐ 2 Chron. 6:12-42	☐ Ezek. 30:20 -31:18	☐ John 11:28-54
16	☐ 2 Chron. 7	☐ Ezek. 32	☐ John 11:55-12:19
17	☐ 2 Chron. 8, 9	☐ Ezek. 33	☐ John 12:20-50
18	☐ 2 Chron. 10, 11	☐ Ezek. 34	☐ John 13:1-30
19	☐ 2 Chron. 12, 13	☐ Ezek. 35:1 -36:15	☐ John 13:31-14:14
20	☐ 2 Chron. 14, 15	☐ Ezek. 36:16-38	☐ John 14:15-31
21	☐ 2 Chron. 16, 17	☐ Ezek. 37	☐ John 15:1-16
22	☐ 2 Chron. 18, 19	☐ Ezek. 38	☐ John 15:17-16:15
23	☐ 2 Chron. 20	☐ Ezek. 39	☐ John 16:16-33
24	☐ 2 Chron. 21, 22	☐ Ezek. 40	☐ John 17
25	☐ 2 Chron. 23, 24	☐ Ezek. 41	☐ John 18:1-27

26	☐ 2 Chron. 25	☐ Ezek. 42	☐ John 18:28-19:16
27	☐ 2 Chron. 26	☐ Ezek. 43	☐ John 19:17-42
28	☐ 2 Chron. 27, 28	☐ Ezek. 44	☐ John 20
29	☐ 2 Chron. 29	☐ Ezek. 45	☐ John 21
30	☐ 2 Chron. 30	☐ Ezek. 46	☐ 1 John 1

DECEMBER

"Now He said to them, "These are My words which I spoke to you while I was still with you, that all things which are written about Me in the Law of Moses and the Prophets and the Psalms must be fulfilled."

(Luke 24:44)

1	☐ 2 Chron. 31	☐ Ezek. 47	☐ 1 John 2:1-17
2	☐ 2 Chron. 32	☐ Ezek. 48	☐ 1 John 2:18-29
3	☐ 2 Chron. 33	☐ Dan. 1	☐ 1 John 3
4	☐ 2 Chron. 34	☐ Dan. 2:1-23	☐ 1 John 4
5	☐ 2 Chron. 35	☐ Dan. 2:24-49	☐ 1 John 5
6	☐ 2 Chron. 36	☐ Dan. 3	☐ 2 John
7	☐ Ezra 1, 2	☐ Dan. 4	☐ 3 John
8	☐ Ezra 3, 4	☐ Dan. 5	☐ Rev. 1
9	☐ Ezra 5	☐ Dan. 6	☐ Rev. 2:1-17
10	☐ Ezra 6	☐ Dan. 7	☐ Rev. 2:18-3:6
11	☐ Ezra 7	☐ Dan. 8	☐ Rev. 3:7-22
12	☐ Ezra 8	☐ Dan. 9	☐ Rev. 4
13	☐ Ezra 9	☐ Dan. 10	☐ Rev. 5
14	☐ Ezra 10	☐ Dan. 11:1-20	☐ Rev. 6
15	☐ Neh. 1, 2	☐ Dan. 11:21-45	☐ Rev. 7
16	☐ Neh. 3	☐ Dan. 12	☐ Rev. 8
17	☐ Neh. 4	☐ Haggai 1	☐ Rev. 9
18	☐ Neh. 5	☐ Haggai 2	☐ Rev. 10
19	☐ Neh. 6	☐ Zech. 1	☐ Rev. 11
20	☐ Neh. 7	☐ Zech. 2, 3	☐ Rev. 12
21	☐ Neh. 8	☐ Zech. 4	☐ Rev. 13
22	☐ Neh. 9	☐ Zech. 5, 6	☐ Rev. 14
23	☐ Neh. 10, 11	☐ Zech. 7	☐ Rev. 15
24	☐ Neh. 12	☐ Zech. 8	☐ Rev. 16
25	☐ Neh. 13	☐ Zech, 9, 10	☐ Rev. 17
26	☐ Esther 1	☐ Zech. 11	☐ Rev. 18
27	☐ Esther 2	☐ Zech 12:1-13:6	☐ Rev. 19:1-10
28	☐ Esther 3, 4	☐ Zech. 13:7 -14:21	☐ Rev. 19:11-20:6
29	☐ Esther 5, 6	☐ Malachi 1:1-2:9	☐ Rev. 20:7-21:8

30 ☐ Esther 7, 8   ☐ Malachi 2:10   ☐ Rev. 21:9-22:5
                        -3:6
31 ☐ Esther 9, 10   ☐ Malachi 3:7-4:6 ☐ Rev. 22:6-21

9 781607 916963